WITHDRAWN

Numbers at the Park: 1-10

by CHARLES GHIGNA

illustrated by AG JATKOWSKA

WITHDRAWN

PICTURE WINDOW BOOKS

a capstone imprint

 **child swinging in the morning light.**

3

2 children flying a big red kite.

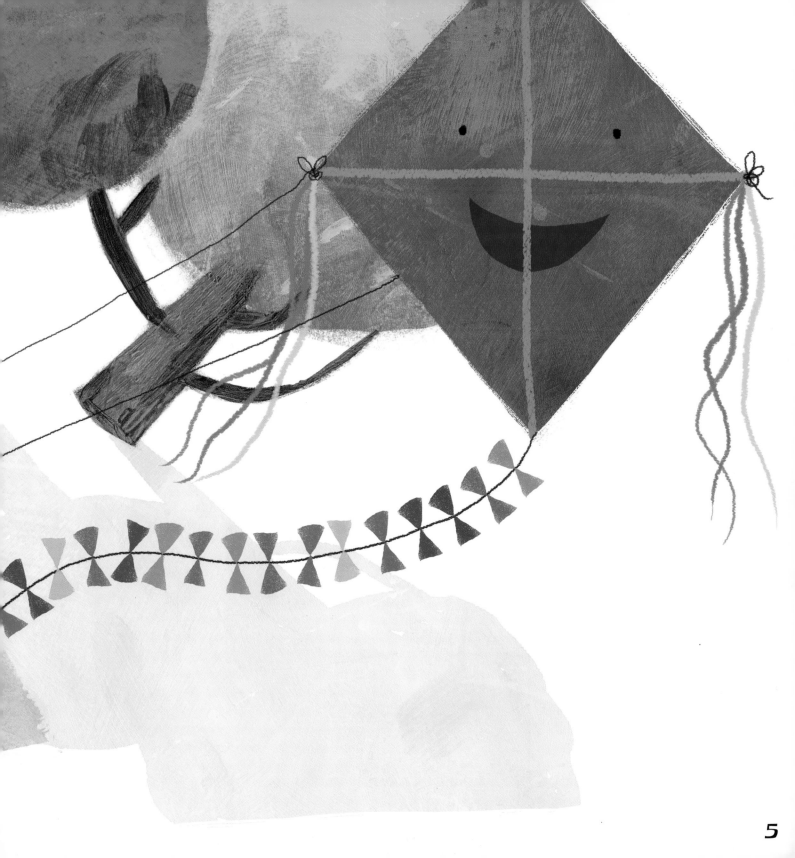

3 children riding on a carousel.

 **4** children ringing
a bright silver bell.

9

5 children playing with puppets on a stage.

 children dancing across this page!

7 children blowing bubbles in the park.

8 children chasing fireflies in the dark.

9 children painting pictures
of the moon.

10 children singing a bedtime tune.

It's fun to count our numbers.
Let's count them once again.
It's fun to count our numbers—
Our numbers 1 to 10!

READ MORE

Capote, Lori. *Monster Knows Numbers.* North Mankato, Minn.: Picture Window Books, 2013.

Rey, H. A. *Curious George Learns to Count from 1 to 100.* Boston: Houghton Mifflin, 2005.

Scarry, Richard. *Richard Scarry's Best Counting Book Ever.* New York: Sterling, 2010.

INTERNET SITES

FactHound offers a safe, fun way to find Internet sites related to this book. All of the sites on FactHound have been researched by our staff.

Here's all you do:

Visit *www.facthound.com*

Type in this code: 9781404883086

Check out projects, games and lots more at
www.capstonekids.com

Look for all the books in the series:

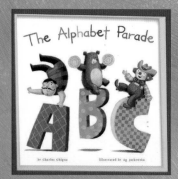

For Charlotte and Christopher

Editor: Shelly Lyons
Designer: Ashlee Suker
Art Director: Nathan Gassman
Production Specialist: Laura Manthe
The illustrations in this book were created digitally.

Picture Window Books are published by Capstone,
1710 Roe Crest Drive, North Mankato, Minnesota 56003
www.capstonepub.com

Library of Congress Cataloging-in-Publication Data
Ghigna, Charles.
Numbers at the park : 1-10 / by Charles Ghigna ; illustrated by
Ag Jatkowska.
pages cm. — (My little school house)
Summary: "Introduces the numbers 1 through 10 through fun,
poetic text."— Provided by publisher.
Audience: Pre-school, excluding K.
Includes bibliographical references.
ISBN 978-1-4048-8308-6 (library binding)
ISBN 978-1-4795-1898-2 (ebook PDF)
1. Number concept—Juvenile literature. 2. Numerals—Juvenile
literature. 3. Counting—Juvenile literature. I. Jatkowska, Ag, illustrator.
II. Title.
QA141.3.G48 2013
513.5'5—dc23
2013006270

Printed in the United States of America in North Mankato, Minnesota.
032013   007223CGF13

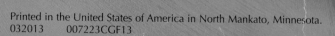